BUILD YOUR BEST BRAIN

Building Habits Today for When Stuff Hits the Fan Tomorrow

JOHN F. EDWARDS, CSP

Copyright © 2024
John F. Edwards
The Edwards Groups, LLC
BUILD YOUR BEST BRAIN
Building Habits Today for When Stuff
Hits the Fan Tomorrow
All rights reserved.

No part of this publication may be reproduced, distributed, or transmitted in any form or by any means, including photocopying, recording, or other electronic or mechanical methods, without the prior written permission of the author, except in the case of brief quotations embodied in critical reviews and certain other non-commercial uses permitted by copyright law.

John F. Edwards
The Edwards Groups, LLC
Apostolos Publishing
North Carolina, United States
Editor: Meagan Wullschleger

Printed Worldwide
First Printing 2024
First Edition 2024

10 9 8 7 6 5 4 3 2 1

ISBN: 978-1-7367660-0-2
Hard Cover ISBN: 978-1-7367660-2-6
e-book ISBN: 978-1-7367660-1-9

Although the author and publisher have made every effort to ensure that the information in this book was correct at the time of publication, the author and publisher do not assume and hereby disclaim any liability to any person or entity with respect to any loss or incidental or consequential damages caused, or alleged to have been caused, directly or indirectly, by the information contained herein, whether resulting from negligence, accident, or any other cause. If you are experiencing significant mental or physical challenges to your well-being, we highly recommend that you seek professional advice or counseling. This book is not intended to replace professional or medical advice.

Dedication

Like so many people, I have had amazing bosses, and I have had a few that have been the opposite. This book is dedicated to amazing bosses.

From my first national sales leader to the seven incredible bosses that I had at my last Fortune 100 Aerospace and Defense company and a couple of fantastic leaders in between, I learned so much and grew so much. I still reflect on the early days of my career when my success exceeded my maturity and cognitive development. The earlier leaders in my young career were precisely what I needed to hold me morally and ethically accountable. To help me clearly understand where the guardrails were yet fully supporting me and my success.

They helped me to better identify what I was looking for in future leaders. People who were more like them and more like who I would like to be. Over my decades-long corporate career, I would define an amazing leader as someone who supports and rejoices in other people's success versus being intimidated or threatened by it. I am so grateful that I had quite a few of those.

Some of their quotes will resonate with me forever, such as "Hire 10s and then get out of their way." "Do all you can do, and then when you've done all you can do… that's all you can do." "The only person that wins the rat race, John… is a rat." Oh, there were so many more quotes. These fantastic leaders were shaping me, my thinking, and ultimately, my results. And now, one of my favorite personal statements to share with leaders around the world is, "The most important job of a leader is the development of his or her people."

Oh sure, it was not always that rosy. I had narcissistic bosses and racist leaders who would much rather see me fail than succeed. But that's a story for another book. Today, I chose to remain focused on all those who poured into me so that I could, one day, prayerfully try to help others.

OTHER BOOKS BY THIS AUTHOR

(available on Amazon):

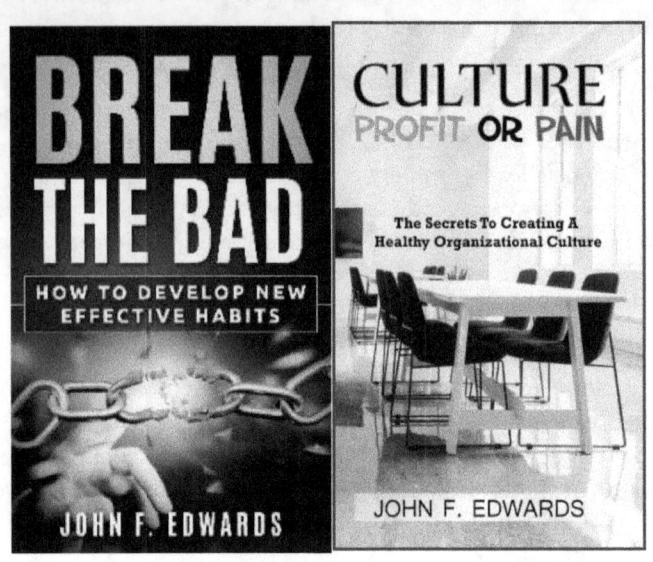

Table of Contents

Chapter 1: Introduction 3
    Why I Wrote This Book 3
    Itchy Moments 4
    Resiliency and your brain 6
    Allostasis 7
Chapter 2: The Problem 13
    Rate of Change 13
    The Prediction Machine 14
Chapter 3: Choose Your Purpose 19
    Personal Mission Statements 19
    My Why 20
    Dimensional Priorities 21
    Clarity of mission 24
    Types of Well-being 26
    Make Plans 28
    Clarity in the Fog 29
    Clarity of Questions 32
    Building Relationships 34
    The B-Plan 38
Chapter 4: Choose Your Program 47
    Messaging 47
    Let's be Deliberate About Being Deliberate 52
    Reset 57
Chapter 5: Choose Your Place 63
    Environment 63
    Physical Space 65
    When 68
    Personal Board of Trustees 72
Conclusion 77
About The Edwards Groups, LLC 79
More about John 81

"To be yourself in a world that is constantly trying to make you something else is the greatest accomplishment."

- often attributed to Ralph Waldo Emerson.

Chapter 1

Introduction

Why I Wrote This Book

The genesis of this book started when I was humbled with a standing ovation. I had just finished presenting to a live audience in New York when the entire auditorium rose to its feet. A few days later, it occurred to me that I should write this stuff down into a book. If live audiences find value in the presentation, I wondered if a reader might as well.

The contemporary version of this speech was reborn in January of 2021. I was in my video studio in Northern Virginia, finalizing the charts for a keynote I was preparing. The audience was going to be healthcare professionals who were struggling with navigating the significant stressors associated with the pandemic lockdown.

It was clear that the stressors that were weighing them down were going to be around for years. So, I decided that the best way to help would be to provide research-based strategies to build their resilience versus only focusing on handling the current stressors.

Since then, this topic has become our most requested speech or workshop content. In a world riddled with conflicts as diverse as the cultures that grace our planet, I should not be surprised that there's a growing demand for insights on enhancing our cognitive abilities.

So, as they say in the United States, "buckle up" because we're here to transform those brain cells into a dream team ready to tackle the challenges of our complex world. Grab your thinking cap, paper, pen, pencil, or even a crayon. Because together, we will build brains so brilliant that they will outshine a disco ball at a New Year's Eve party!

Itchy Moments

What would you say to your past self if you could travel back in time? Of course, we might be tempted to warn ourselves about a few personal things: "Don't get bangs!" or "Just because it looked easy in an online video doesn't mean that cutting your own hair is going to be a good idea!"

Once we've given our past selves a stern hairdo lecture and stashed away the golden lottery numbers (because, let's be honest, we're practical dreamers), what would you focus on next? If it were me, I would tell myself how to better handle upcoming stressful situations. I would do this because I know I would see my anxiety levels drop faster than a rock in a well. I would give my past self a sneak peek of the future and reveal incredible insights into navigating life's twists and turns. It would be like having a personal crystal ball dispensing handy life advice. A cheat sheet to life's greatest lesson.

For better or for worse, we cannot yet bend the space-time continuum. Believe me, I have tried. More than once.

Since we cannot go back and give ourselves specific advice, we need to build cognitive resilience to successfully navigate what lies ahead. So, how can we help our brains to become more resilient without arming them with specific knowledge of the future?

This book will explore a framework to Build Your Best Brain. You will be given three strategies to reinvigorate and rejuvenate your cognitive capacity. I call them Purpose, Program, and Place. I will also provide proven applications for implementing these secrets to help you train your brain to adjust to unpredictable, complex circumstances.

It is all about leaning into and accelerating your success. The practical insights offered here will help you to apply these concepts to your life in a powerful way. And that is why I wrote this book.

So, let's dive in. In this world of self-improvement, there are moments that I've lovingly dubbed "itchy moments." These are the times when you might feel a little uncomfortable. For example, it might occur when you are reminded that your current habit may not be the best thing for you to do.

You might be binge-watching a horror show, and about to grab your fourth slice of pizza, and all of a sudden, that uncomfortable thought enters your brain. Your streaming service asks if you are still watching, and you have to pause to ask yourself, "Wait, should I really be eating another slice? This moment where your brain triggers a slightly uncomfortable... maybe even itchy sense that makes you cognitively squirm for a second. Yup, that pause is an itchy moment.

Our natural tendency is not to lean into these moments. On the contrary, we might find ourselves eager to dismiss them so that we can rapidly return to our comfortable sense of being. But I encourage you to pay attention because itchy moments often present some of our best learning opportunities. In their apparent discomfort, they harbor the potential for intellectual and personal growth of the most exhilarating kind.

Suppose you find this happening while reading this book. At that moment, I invite you to lean into them, knowing that the strategies you are learning are designed to help your brain build resilience and contribute to your well-being.

Resiliency and your brain

From a neuroscience point of view, cognitive resilience is like your brain's superpower for bouncing back from tough times and challenges. It is directly tied to your overall well-being. Think of it as your brain's ability to stay strong, adapt, and push forward even when things get tricky. Just like a rubber band that stretches and then returns to its original shape, a resilient brain can handle stress, setbacks, and changes in a way that keeps you going strong.

Your brain is central to your ability to navigate and recover from stress. Your brain's ability to link and collaborate between various neural networks determines whether you will have extraordinary resiliency or if you will be maladapted to the changes in your environment. In fact, your brain goes through structural changes in response to stress-related hormones.[1] To counter the negative impact on your brain, you must work deliberately to build that muscle today for the stressors it will experience tomorrow.

To build your best brain, you need a framework that encourages you to develop daily habits for resilience. I will provide a research-based framework that shows you what to add to your routines and what to take out. You need specific steps that you can

---

[1] McEwen, B. (2013). The Brain on Stress. Perspectives on Psychological Science, 8, 673 - 675. https://doi.org/10.1177/1745691613506907.

immediately implement, and I am grateful for the opportunity to share some with you.

The human brain is an amazing, powerful machine that you can harness for your benefit in ambiguous, uncertain, ever-changing, or even overwhelming situations. That is what cognitive resilience is all about.

Most well-being strategies deal with managing current stress or navigating your existing challenges. While that is very important, our approach to Build Your Best Brain will give you the tools to develop daily habits that build resiliency today for the inevitable stuff that might hit the fan tomorrow.

It is much better to train your brain today than to let tomorrow's stressors sneak up on you like a ninja in a library. We want to help you become a mental athlete by sharpening your cognitive swords, doing brain push-ups, and mastering the art of cognitive resilience.

Resiliency can be improved by empowering and training the brain today to respond well to the unknown challenges of tomorrow. Much of the research indicates that focusing on your cognitive resilience will help you cope with stress and enhance problem-solving, workplace performance, and physical health.

Allostasis

We are limited because we only have so much cognitive capacity. Think of a pitcher of your favorite beverage. When I first relocated to this charming region in the south of the United States, I held the naive belief that sweet tea was merely tea with a dash of sugar. I was sorely mistaken! Southerners don't just make sweet tea; they make magic in a glass. It's like they're brewing liquid sunshine with a hefty dose of Southern charm. I mean, they take sweet tea so seriously; it's practically a way of life. So, when I speak to live audiences, I naturally use a pitcher of Southern iced tea for my illustration.

Now it's your turn to imagine a pitcher of your favorite beverage. Maybe your imaginary pitcher is full of delightful, iced tea with lemons, or perhaps it's homemade fruit punch. Go ahead and imagine we are talking about your favorite refreshing beverage.

Now, imagine pouring yourself a glass out of your pitcher every time your brain has to navigate a source of stress. You might have to pour some out when solving a work-related issue early in the morning. Then, pour another glass when you hear a disturbing update on the news. Pour another glass when you arrive home to a stressful family conversation. Any remaining beverage can be poured out of your pitcher as you check the calendar for tomorrow, and the stress piles on, leaving you without any more sweat tea.

So, what happens to your empty pitcher? How is it refilled for the next day? When we pour out our pitcher repeatedly, it is the equivalent of depleting your brain battery.

We become overloaded with no resources left to handle even more minor stressors. When we learn how to reframe our perspective, a remarkable transformation takes place. A transformation that allows us to refill our pitchers with resiliency. We don't want to just limit how much is poured out of the pitcher; we want to also develop ways to refill the pitcher. That leads us into a conversation about Allostasis.

Allostasis is a physiological process in which the body regulates the use of energy to adapt to stressors in a changing environment. In other words, our brain and body combine and coordinate to create stability in adjusting to external stressors. This process is linked to our ability to cope and adapt. There is a direct correlation between how well our body navigates chronic stress and our immune system's ability to keep us healthy.

Think of your brain and body combination as operating like an automobile combustible engine. Multiple systems are operating at any given time, all working to handle whatever comes along. Your brain is in the driver's seat, taking in all the information and acting like your GPS to find the best way to navigate.

Allostasis is like your engine's adaptive response system when an unexpected stressor pops up. The engine revs up and sends cortisol and adrenaline into the system. Your senses get sharper, and your heart rate increases. Now, you are ready to kick into high gear. You would not want to drive your car all week in that heightened state, nor would you want your body to be in that state constantly.

Allostatic load refers to the consequence of being in that heightened stress state. This is the process of pouring a lot out of the pitcher of your favorite drink. If we pour out too often or for too long, our allostatic load can result in long-term medical implications, including permanently altering our brains.[2]

Furthermore, allostatic load reduces our ability to deal with whatever stressors may occur tomorrow. At the more extreme end, post-traumatic stress disorder (PTSD) has been linked in numerous research writings to the challenge of allostatic load.[3] That is why it is vitally important that we find ways to refill our pitcher every day.

We know that news outlets, social media, and other inputs that surround us may be contributing to our brain's overloading. When our pitcher is emptied, we experience a brain drain. Brain drain

---
[2] Peters A, McEwen BS, Friston K (September 2017). "Uncertainty and stress: Why it causes diseases and how it is mastered by the brain". *Progress in Neurobiology*.
[3] McEwen, B. (2003). Mood disorders and allostatic load. Biological Psychiatry.

takes effect when we no longer have the cognitive capacity to make wise decisions that align with our personal purpose. Those are the days you find yourself yelling at the barista who asked how your day was going. You are not able to process the information; your brain is overloaded. It's like trying to fit a T-Rex into a Mini Cooper.

Considering all of this, what can we do to combat the competition for our attention? Fret not, for within you lies the power to reprogram your allostasis programming code.

Think of it as giving your brain a much-needed daily software update. You'll regain the cognitive capacity to make wiser decisions that align with your personal purpose, and the barista will thank you for it!

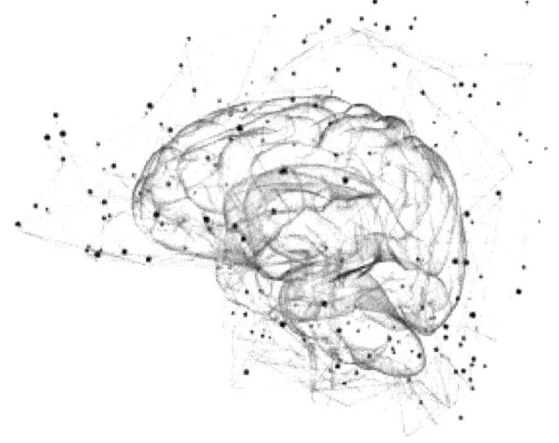

"The most difficult thing is the decision to act; the rest is merely tenacity."

- Amelia Earhart.

Chapter 2

The Problem

Rate of Change

Let's start by telling you something you may already know. The rate of change in the world today is faster and more furious than ever before. It's like trying to keep up with a caffeinated hummingbird on roller skates! Our brains really don't like it.

During my presentations on the topic of change, there's always that one eager soul who raises their hand and poses the age-old question: "Why is change so problematic for us now, even though it has been around since the invention of the wheel?" And they are right. Change has been around since... well, forever.

We had an acceleration during the Renaissance era, and then the 20th Century thrust us into the fastest pace of change we have ever seen.[4] It's like the world looked at my fellow Jamaican athlete, Usain Bolt, and said, "Hold my coffee!" One minute, we're learning about the latest smartphone, and the next, our toasters have become sentient beings demanding gluten-free bread!

---

[4] Kreis-Engelhardt, B. (1999). Zusammenfassung und Perspektiven. , 175-179. https://doi.org/10.1007/978-3-322-97797-7_7.

We can think about change as occurring on three levels: organizational, personal, or social. Organizational change would involve changes related to the workplace, while personal change would be more aligned with changes in our individual lives. Social changes would be more about our peer group, which would include everything from family to any other larger group with which we identify.

So, no matter whether personal, social, or organizational, the increase in pace for the frequency and magnitude of changes impacts our cognitive capability and increases stress. Notwithstanding the significant difference in the brain for highly threatening negative changes like the loss of a job, death of a loved one, and divorce, just to name a few.

Has this been true for you? Have you noticed an increase in the pace and magnitude of changes that impact your life? Have you seen greater fatigue, stress, and possibly an impact on productivity? If so, please know that this is normal, and you can do something about it. Let's spend a moment understanding some of what is occurring in our brains.

The Prediction Machine

Our brains love predictability. The human brain is a prediction machine! Some of you were taught that the brain is a thinking machine. While that is true, I would add that the brain thinks in order to predict. It is a survival mechanism to want to know and understand what will happen next.

Unpredictability is like a brain's internal horror story. It will make something up if it doesn't know what will happen. Let's say you just got a text that says, "We need to talk." What thought immediately comes to your mind? Were you thinking, "Oh golly, I bet this is about giving me an early birthday present!" Neither does your brain assume that they want to talk to you about the difference between ice cream and frozen yogurt. Although I firmly believe that would be a conversation best done with samples! But, I digress…

Back to the human brain: our very own personal drama factory! You see, in the absence of information, our brain becomes the master storyteller, but it seems to have misplaced its comedy script. Instead, it's all about the thriller and horror genres. Give your brain a tiny bit of uncertainty, and suddenly, it's creating a blockbuster where you're the star of a disaster movie!

When you hear a strange noise in the middle of the night, your brain doesn't think, "Oh, it must be a cute little kitten playing." No, it's more like, "Alert! It's definitely a band of rogue ninjas trying to steal your grandma's secret jerk pork recipe!" Our brains never seem to make up positive stuff. It's always a worst-case scenario.

Unfortunately, when our brains do that to us, we will literally have a physical reaction; our palms get sweaty, our hearts race, and our breathing patterns change. Uncertainty, ambiguity, and complexity make our brains very uncomfortable. If you think about some of the seasons of your life that have been the most challenging and stressful, they will likely have inconsistency and unpredictability in common. When we feel we are able to have a simple, clear expectation of the future, our stress levels often reduce dramatically. The brain is constantly evaluating all of the sensory inputs bombarding it so that it can prioritize which pieces are most important for making predictions.[5]

Take the COVID-19 quarantine period, for example. Stress, anxiety, and depression rates skyrocketed because of fear of the unknown. We did not have the level of predictability, clarity, or

---

[5] Clark, A. (2015). Radical predictive processing. *Southern Journal of Philosophy*.

simplicity required for our brains to operate comfortably. The human brain needs resiliency fuel to avoid becoming overwhelmed.

You can grow your resilience capacity, which will be the focus of the next few chapters. What do I need to do to align the powerful neural networks of my brain so that I can develop habits and practices that promote greater cognitive capacity? The answer is in the Three-P-Framework of Purpose, Program, and Place.

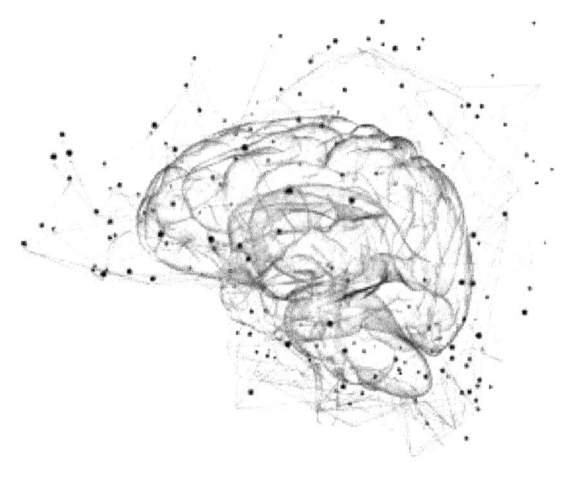

"He who has a why to live can bear almost any how."

-Friedrich Nietzsche

Chapter 3

Choose Your Purpose

Personal Mission Statements

We define personal purpose as a deliberate and thoughtful articulation of who you want to authentically be, how you want to consistently show up, and how you will contribute to others. Studies reveal that having a purpose helps the brain to predict and manage the future.[6] When we have clarity about our purpose, the brain will do a better job regulating our body's energy and giving us some coherence in a continuously changing environment. This increased ability to manage energy expenditure allows us to be better at adapting to changes.[7]

---

[6] Halkjelsvik, T., & Jørgensen, M. (2018). How We Predict Time Usage.
[7] Nierenberg, A. (2019). What's Our Brain for Anyway? *Psychiatric Annals*.

My Why

Everything begins with knowing your WHY. Why are you in your current job? Now, if it's because they are the only company that would hire you after that incident back in '92, well...

But seriously, why do you do what you do? A mentor once told me: "Figure out what you love to do, and then do it so well that someone will pay you to do it. Then, you'll never work another day in your life." Over the years, I have come to discover and rediscover the power behind that piece of advice.

This is truly the secret sauce to finding joy in our work. It is a marriage between our passion and our purpose and how we spend our time making a living. The research is very clear about what happens to our brains when our work and joy intersect. You may not be surprised by any of this. Joy in our work drives positive mental, emotional, and behavioral benefits.[8] When joy, the job, and our purpose are united, brain areas that process rewards, engagement, and stress reduction are lit up like a Times Square Christmas Tree.

What is it that drives you to do what you do? Pause here and ponder that question.

Make a decision to articulate why you do what you do, and then you'll be able to give your brain a blueprint for expectations. This brings clarity to decision-making and increases intrinsic motivation. Additionally, your clarity allows your allies, sponsors, and mentors to better know how they can contribute to your success in a meaningful way. When you choose your purpose, you move your brain toward the predictability it naturally seeks.

---

[8] Costello, E. (2010). Grand Challenges in Child and Neurodevelopmental Psychiatry.

Dimensional Priorities

Here in Western-educated countries, we do not tend to think about our personal purpose. Organizations focus on purpose, which is why they have mission statements. There is a well-thought-out purpose for an organization to exist. Corporate websites are littered with information about "Our Vision," "Mission Statement," and "Core Values." You're probably well aware of many such statements in your own workplace. However, are you as familiar with your personal purpose?

While organizations have mission statements, individuals should as well. We must each have a purpose that is articulated in a written statement. It has to be clear and concise. "I exist to accelerate the success of other people." That is my personal purpose. It reflects my individual core values, the reason for my existence, and my "why." That level of clarity changes everything. It leads to cleaner and faster decisions and fewer internal cognitive conflicts.

Writing down a personal purpose statement promotes rich cognitive encoding, stimulates the creative process, and activates the memory portions of your brain. Thinking about it is not enough; we must also write it down. While typing your personal statement into an electronic device is better than just thinking about it, research indicates that mechanically writing it down leads to higher activation in specific brain regions.[9] When you know your purpose and write it down, it adds clarity to everything you do.

Start with: "Who do you want to be?" Everyone has multiple identities. I am a father, a husband, and a grandfather. I am also a man, a man of color, and I am from the Caribbean. Additionally,

---

[9] Umejima, K., Ibaraki, T., Yamazaki, T., & Sakai, K. (2021). Paper Notebooks vs. Mobile Devices: Brain Activation Differences During Memory Retrieval.

I'm a speaker, musician, former professional athlete, and coach. You get the idea; there are multiple perspectives on our identities, and I call them Identity Dimensions. Let me ask you to do the following activity right where you are.

1. Make a list of all of your Identity Dimensions. Go ahead, I'll wait. (insert elevator music here).

2. Now that you have done that, identify the top 5 that are the most important to you. Just circle them in no particular order.

This prioritization helps us deal with multiple issues. I call this Dimensional Priorities. We can filter our choices about how we choose to show up based on our most important identities, but we can only do that after we've established clarity about what those identity priorities are. Knowing who we want to be helps prevent us from becoming who we don't want to be.

When our brains are significantly taxed, we might sacrifice our higher priorities for our lower priorities. When stress triggers an amygdala reaction, we often fail to process which filters are most important because we lack the cognitive capacity for that level of prioritization. For example, if my identity as a father is circled on my list, I have to ask myself why I would get into a heated argument with one of my children over politics. Politics is nowhere to be found on my Dimensional Priority list, so why do I let it compromise something that is identified as a very important component of who I want to be?

Maybe you also prioritized family dimensions such as sibling, child, or parent. Yet, a lack of intentional focus on what we have identified as important personal dimensions can often lead us into a conflict that costs us more than we ever wanted to pay. Sometimes, it makes sense to place the relationship we have with someone else as much higher than proving a point or winning an argument. A heightened awareness of dimensional priorities also helps us in the moment to determine how to best respond to any stimulus that activates the amygdala threat mechanism.

As you may already know, the amygdala is the area of the brain involved with emotions. It links them to memories and decision-making, among other functions. In a more heightened state of arousal, the amygdala activates our threat response system, also known as fight, flight, or freeze. Consequently, you and I may find it challenging to initiate a rational response when our amygdala is highly activated.

In situations like this, we say and do things we may regret later. It's the part of the brain that leaps before it looks, turning us into masters of the verbal faux pas. For example, there you are, commenting on someone's adventurous new hairstyle with the subtlety of a bull in a China shop.

Later, you replay your words in horror, utterly embarrassed by your response. Remember, it's not you; it's your amygdala, high on the thrill of chaos. This tiny brain tyrant can make a mountain from a molehill. This is where we can compromise what is most important to us by negatively reacting to something less important.

This is what happens when we show up to others in ways inconsistent with how we truly wish to show up. Situations like this create Dimensional Dissonance in our brains. I call this Dimensional Dissonance because it is a variable of cognitive dissonance.

Dissonance occurs in our brains when one construct or cognition is in conflict with another, and the more important to us they are, the more significant the impact on your brain.[10] That is why the exercise you did above is so important. It brings clarity to

---

[10] Festinger, L. (1957). A Theory of Cognitive Dissonance.

the PFC and informs decision-making so that it more closely aligns with your own personal core values and your articulated "why."

Clarity of mission

Your neurons are constantly doing remarkable things to help you stay balanced. Your axons and synapses function on a cellular level to balance your body. What happens when you use your personal mission statement to make decisions is different than when you allow things to happen without intentional metacognition. This is the difference between reactive thinking and deliberate decision-making. When you know your WHY, an activation occurs in parts of your brain that were not previously engaged.

Think about the networks in your brain as if they were constellations. Visualize your neurons as an interconnected network of stars. Many smaller stars make up something greater as they connect to each other. Often, we tap into various areas of the brain to blend our past experiences, values, and feelings to make sense of something. We access various neural networks to help us make meaning of our world.

Let me give you an example. If I say "cat," what comes into your mind? Maybe you had a childhood pet that you loved. You know, those furry, lovable things from which we draw joy, comfort, and a test of our reflexes. In a weak moment of needing love, you picked up that soft cat with the anticipation of a dopamine rush. With the neural wiring of its ancient ancestors, the cat picks the most inappropriate and painfully embarrassing way to touch your face with its claws.

Consequently, when I say the word "cat," you instinctively touch your cheek right where the faithful incident occurred so many years ago. All I did was say the word, and your brain made sense of it. It filled in the missing pieces and either created or recalled a story. For me, I would recall both my first childhood feline and the last one I had in my adult years. Both illicit warm emotions for me as I lived with them for years until their end of life.

Maybe, instead of a childhood pet, your brother worked for the company Caterpillar. You're familiar with the company that makes machines, tractors, and construction equipment. You've seen their big yellow machines working on the construction site as you drive past. If that's you, you probably might hear the word "cat" and immediately think of your hard-working sibling who has put 15 years into developing his trade. Again, just one word, and your brain fills in the rest.

The way that our brains make sense of individual words is through a network. When you hear a word, your brain searches for the network that contextualizes it and then processes it accordingly. In essence, the brain uses shortcuts to form quick narratives. One word is never just one isolated word; it is a whole constellation of neurons.

When you zoom out of specific constellations to view the whole sky, the brain can be partitioned into seven different networks. Each network is either responsible for or plays a cooperative role in processing input and stimulating output. Motivation in our brains is stimulated by various networks.

Motivation to action is associated with stimulating the midbrain dopaminergic neurons, among others.[11] This is called the MDN network. Stimulating your MDN and its cooperative systems activates a network that secretes more epinephrine, norepinephrine,

---

[11] Hassan, A., & Benarroch, E. (2015). Heterogeneity of the midbrain dopamine system.

oxytocin, and other hormones that are powerful motivators. Other authors and speakers refer to this system as your "Why."

So, when you figure out your WHY, you align your neural networks to help you develop perseverance, take on challenges without feeling defeated, and learn how to grow with resilience. Figuring out some of the things discussed in this book will activate neural activity that allows the amazing and powerful non-conscious part of your brain to help accelerate your success and build cognitive resilience. Knowing your purpose will enable you to press on despite obstacles, challenges, and distractions as you make big and small decisions.

Types of Well-being

There are two types of well-being that we can understand as motivating factors in our cognitive capacity. Hedonic meaning is fleeting and linked to a pleasant sensation. It is often defined by a more immediate sense of pleasure, like when you purchase something. However, there is no deeper, noble meaning associated with this.

Baking during the COVID-19 stay-at-home order is an excellent example of this. So many of us were searching for some form of pleasure to help manage the stress associated with the pandemic. According to the Hershey Company, approximately 30% of us acquired new baking skills during this time. The Wall Street Journal[12] published an article stating that sales of baking supplies and mixes rose 25% in 2020.

I know my daughter baked her fair share of bread, cakes, and other delicious distractions while stuck in the house. So, as it turns

---

[12] The Wall Street Journal. Is Baking's Pandemic Popularity Just a Flash in the Pan? (May 25, 2021)

out, baking was something that a lot of people "kneaded" as their way of "rising" to the occasion.

Sorry, I couldn't help myself. But I digress.

Eudaimonic meaning, on the other hand, is linked to deeper, lasting well-being. Eudaimonia is a word that comes from the Greek. It means happiness and flourishing and may be spelled in the literature in a few different ways, including eudaemonia or eudemonia. Aristotle found this to be essential and identified it as a moral component that is key to our ultimate purpose or our "chief good." The Aristotelian perspective is that to attain eudaimonia requires a virtuous life characterized by healthy relationships, generosity, courage, and justice.[13]

The terms eudaimonic and well-being are linked. Some research shows that self-employed individuals report higher eudemonic well-being.[14] This may not be a surprise given the level of autonomy and perceptions of meaningfulness associated with that type of work. Being your own boss helps you define your own purpose both inside and outside of work.

When you articulate your purpose, you arouse the part of the brain that is stimulated by meaning and self-value, and subsequently, your brain increases its resiliency. When we are grounded in eudaimonic meaning, we have an improved ability to bounce back from stressors. There is a deep, lasting anchor in our decision-making that we can leverage to make better and sometimes faster decisions. Thus, it is essential to take the time to articulate the noble purpose behind all that we do.

---

[13] Bryce, A., (1028). Finding meaning through work. University of Sheffield, Department of Economics

[14] Stephan, U., et. al. (2020). Self-employment and eudaimonic well-being: Energized by meaning, enabled by societal legitimacy.

We access accelerated transformation when we identify our purpose and then share it with others. Studies reveal that articulating and sharing our purpose with others leads to improved goal attainment, higher motivation, and positive shifts in relationships.[15] It is not just about thinking through our personal WHY but also about communicating it to others.

We are all here for a reason and have been given the skills to accelerate bringing our personal purpose to life. What lights your fire the most? You are here to use what passion, to solve what problem(s), and to benefit whom? This formula is not my own; however, I have seen it used a multitude of times as a template to get a personal mission statement started. Please pause to capture your thoughts.

Make Plans

Earlier in the book, we noted that the purpose of the brain as a prediction machine. Well, one of the ways we can equip our brains to handle unpredictability is to have something to look forward to. When you have something to hope for and look forward to, something to countdown towards on the calendar, it gives your brain a positive focus.

For example, maybe you've always wanted to go to that indoor skydiving place. For me, it is looking forward to bringing my grandchildren to the beach. It's the mental equivalent of finding money in your old jeans, which is a delightful surprise that boosts your mood instantly. You don't even have to wait for the activity for the brain boost!

---

[15] Huang, S., Broniarczyk, S., Zhang, Y., & Beruchashvili, M. (2015). From Close to Distant: The Dynamics of Interpersonal Relationships in Shared Goal Pursuit.

The benefit to your brain starts with planning the activity. These anticipated activities work like mental confetti, turning even the dullest days into a 'looking forward to it' parade. They're essential for our sanity, like coffee for the soul. It does not even have to be a big black-tie affair. Looking forward to something you anticipate enjoying can be centered on something as simple as a visit to the spa or hiking your favorite trail.

As long as it is on the calendar and it is a positive event to engage, entertain, or otherwise edify your brain, then it helps build cognitive resilience. When we have activities or events regularly scheduled for our future, it arouses the prefrontal cortex and enhances information-seeking behavior. This, in turn, triggers a dopamine release and activates hippocampal activity.[16]

Dopamine is often referred to as the "feel good" hormone and is linked to motivation and reward. The hippocampus is involved in learning, memory, and emotional behavior. So, you plan something to look forward to, dopamine is released in your hippocampus, and you feel good. Viola!

So then, what are you looking forward to? Maybe now is a good time to pause and make a list of activities or events that you will schedule for the next 6-8 months at intervals that make the most sense for you. What have you not done in a while that would be healthy and positive for you to do again?

Clarity in the Fog

Positive future events can help to pull us out of the daily fog. We live in a world of fog, and we are constantly surrounded by it.

---

[16] Iigaya, K., Hauser, T., Kurth-Nelson, Z., O'Doherty, J., Dayan, P., & Dolan, R. (2020). The value of what's to come: Neural mechanisms coupling prediction error and the utility of anticipation.

The fog is created by endless sensory inputs, and honestly, many of them were specifically designed to attract and distract you. Your brain is constantly being bombarded with messages.

Right now, you are filtering out sensory inputs left and right. Maybe you're ignoring the sound of the HVAC unit running in your office, the skittering of the squirrels in the tree outside your window, the incessant notifications lighting up your phone, and the buzzing of the fluorescent overhead lights.

Your brain is filtering out all that fog simultaneously. Maybe you're ignoring the pitter-patter of your children's feet in the playroom above your head, the barking of the dog outside your home office, the scratchiness of the worn spot in your carpet, and the twinge in your back from how you slept last night. The list of possible sensory inputs is endless.

Unconscious brain activity accounts for more than 90% of total neural activity. The non-conscious part of your brain uses neural mechanisms to prioritize sensory input and determine if there will be a behavioral response from you.[17] Your brain is continually determining what is and is not essential.

It is healthy and necessary for the brain to ignore much of the stimuli because it would otherwise be overwhelming. The brain must screen out stimuli and determine what noise should get through. When you figure out your WHY, you bring clarity to your non-conscious brain in deciding what input to prioritize.

That is why you need to be deliberate about what you teach your brain to focus on. Listen up friends because this is big deal. Your personal purpose is one of the most essential criteria that your

---

[17] Pally, R. (2005). Non-Conscious Prediction and a Role for Consciousness in Correcting Prediction Errors.

brain can use to delineate between important stimuli versus something to ignore.

Another concept that helps us to understand this further is called the reticular activating system (RAS); in other words, the brain will see what you tell it to see. The RAS is a network of neurons linked to attention and arousal and is connected to the midbrain activity we referenced earlier.[18]

The RAS is responsible for many cognitive functions related to awareness and plays a significant role in shaping our survival instinct. It acts like a filter for incoming sensory information, shifting our conscious awareness and attention to only what is important. The RAS is how we know to pay attention to the voice of our boss instead of the buzzing of the HVAC vent.

Yeah, getting that order of prioritization wrong would not be good. I guess you could call the RAS your personal "Mind Bouncer" because it is your brain's way of ensuring that you put what your boss is saying over the musings of a loud, "I need a tune-up" HVAC system, which, let's be honest, is just full of hot air anyway.

Sorry about that joke. These setups are very hard to resist, and I was left unsupervised. But I digress.

The RAS takes what we focus on and creates a filter for it, sifting through the data and presenting only the pieces that are important to us. This happens without us noticing, and the RAS programs itself to work in our favor. When you can harness the potential for your brain to filter information according to your WHY, you will activate and accelerate your success significantly.

---

[18] Kinomura, S., Larsson, J., Gulyás, B., & Roland, P. (1996). Activation by Attention of the Human Reticular Formation and Thalamic Intralaminar Nuclei.

Clarity of Questions

The brain, as a prediction machine, is addicted to questions. Training ourselves to focus on questions helps train the brain to develop the habit of curiosity. The research shows that questions bring clarity to understanding ourselves, human behavior, and social situations. When we develop a curious question-asking brain, it enhances our memory and promotes better decision-making.[19]

Questions tend to activate the release of serotonin in the brain. This encourages more regions of the brain to be involved in processing the question. In essence, when a question is asked, the processing of that question becomes a temporary priority for the brain.

Often, our brains will focus automatically on win-and-lose scenarios. Instead, we can train it to ask: "What would a win/win look like?" This is like the perception shift that is often given as marriage advice. Maybe you've heard it. It sounds something like this: Stop approaching an argument with your significant other with the intent to win the argument. If your focus is to win, that means your partner must lose. Instead, approach an argument as teammates. You are on the same team, which means you both win or you both lose.

Just like viewing a spouse as a teammate instead of an opponent is a radical shift in marital communication, reframing scenarios in your mind as questions will rewire your brain. When asking questions becomes a natural habit, it will contribute to building your best brains. The National Institute of Health states

---

[19] Illes, J., & Borgelt, E. (2009). Brain imaging: Incidental findings: in practice and in person.

that everything we do comes from the questions that stimulate our thinking.[20]

When I was responsible for executive development programs for a Fortune 100 company, I often trained leaders with this mantra: "Be the first to ask a question and the last to make a statement." We can reduce the stress associated with not knowing by embracing the assumption that there is so much more to be learned. The art of curiosity stimulates the brain to a higher level of creativity and critical thinking, thus activating reward circuitry instead of stress circuitry.

Now, if you've ever hung out with a toddler, you might find the idea of curiosity as a source of stress reduction, to be as believable as a unicorn running a marathon. Toddlers, those tiny humans with the energy of a tornado and the persistence of a telemarketer, have perfected the art of asking questions.

Perhaps all we remember about toddlers is how frustrating it was conversing with one who has embarked on a daily "Why-athon." By the time they hit their 400th "why," you're not just questioning the nature of the universe; you are questioning your sanity. It's like being in a never-ending game show, but every question is "Why?" and there are no fabulous prizes, just a headache and a newfound appreciation for silence.

As opposed to curious toddlers, for adults, the art of curiosity is like a gym membership for your brain. Questions stretch your cognitive muscles and stimulate your brain in a way that builds empathy, improves memory, and enhances relationships. Questions help our brains to pause and process in a healthy, effective way.

---

[20] Neirotti R. A. (2021). The importance of asking questions and doing things for a reason.

Building Relationships

We also get smarter when we interact with each other. For example, if John is a six on a hypothetical smartness scale of 1-10, he can never get to a nine without connectivity to another person. If he is isolated, John is maxed out long before he reaches nine or ten. When we are engaged in community with others, our cognitive capacity increases in areas like cognition, learning, mental health, and problem-solving.[21] [22]

Whether you are an introvert or extrovert, building community wherever you go can be positive and powerful for your brain. That does not mean it is easy to do, but it does mean it is necessary. Community fosters healthy brains. Keep in mind that your group does not have to be ten or twenty people, as creating even temporary connections with one other can reap benefits.[23]

This might be hard for you to believe about a professional motivational speaker, but I'm the type of person who has to know the server's name at a restaurant, who will ask strangers random questions, and who talks to people around me in all sorts of different scenarios. I devised creative ways to interact with others, unintentionally embarrassing my children in public when they were teenagers. I suppose you could label me an outgoing, unabashed, embarrassing extrovert.

Accordingly, I once struck up a conversation with the man standing next to me in the buffet line of a hotel in Australia. As our conversation continued, I soon discovered that he was the head coach of the South African cricket team. By the time we reached the end of the buffet line, he had offered me four tickets to the

---

[21] Jacobs, G., Renandya, W., & Power, M. (2016). Student–Student Interaction.
[22] Gashi, S. (2018). Unobtrusive Recognition of Socio-Affective Dynamics During Human Interactions Using Wearables and Smartphones.
[23] Bruhn, J. (2004). The sociology of community connections.

upcoming match between Australia and South Africa. When I later picked up the tickets from the hotel's front desk, it turned out that he had generously left me six tickets.

On my trips to Australia, I would typically be there for a week or two to conduct training for a cohort of corporate leaders in an executive development program. I was there by myself, so the coach had left me more than enough tickets. That morning, I kicked off my training session with a simple task: finding volunteers to go with me to watch a cricket match. You'd think I was offering free tickets to a space shuttle launch because in exactly 3.42 seconds flat (yes, I timed it), I had five friends who suddenly discovered newfound freedom in their schedules. It's amazing how quickly 'busy' evaporates when cricket and freebies are involved.

So there I was, a spectator with VIP tickets from the South African team, yet also a trainer embraced by Australian leaders. As the game started, I found myself in a dilemma... Who to cheer for? I mean, one minute you're sipping tea with the Aussies, the next you're learning how to say "Golden Duck" in South African. It's like being at a family reunion and forgetting whose side of the family you're on right before the annual tug-of-war or canoe race.

As it turned out, it did not matter. Competitive camaraderie at the two Australian athletic events I have attended over the years is quite collegial and impressive. When one of the South African batters achieved an extraordinary statistical accomplishment, everyone rose to their feet and applauded, regardless of which team they were supporting.

It was like watching rival fans at a Dallas Cowboys versus New York Giants football game suddenly decide to do a group hug. Don't laugh at me because I have endless hope. It could happen one day… maybe in a parallel universe. But I digress.

Back to the cricket match. The spirit of sportsmanship was so thick in the air that you could spread it on a cracker. Their respect for the community of the sport was greater than their respect for their individual teams. The sense of community, mutual respect, and sheer joy of the game were like a stress relief seminar but, of course, with more beer and hot dogs.

This sense of community is a powerful catalyst for inducing high performance, lower stress, and greater cognitive well-being. Yet here in North America and elsewhere, we have become a society of expert ignorers. Walk down any street, and you'll see people so glued to their phones they wouldn't notice a clown on a unicycle juggling flamingos. We pop our headphones in, keep our eyes down, stay in our little bubbles, and practically bump into lamp posts to avoid even eye contact with each other.

This modern tango of dodging real-life interactions is not just making us socially awkward; it's cranking up our stress levels and chipping away at our resilience like a woodpecker on a caffeine buzz. Oh my golly, we are missing so many opportunities to connect with others, and it is depleting our brains. As our obsession with smart devices grows, our ability to look up and recognize the existence of another human being has shrunk faster than the balloon at a kid's birthday party.

It is making us unknowingly pour way too much out of our pitchers.[24] Remember when a simple "hello" from a stranger could make your day? Let's face it, life's too short to spend it pretending the person next to you doesn't exist. Scenes like this add stress to your brain.

---

[24] Chu, J., Qaisar, S., Shah, Z., & Jalil, A. (2021). Attention or Distraction? The Impact of Mobile Phone on Users' Psychological Well-Being. *Frontiers in Psychology*.

All that screen time often leads to a lack of meaningful human connection. Our brains are wired to thrive on social interaction, not just emojis and likes. So, when we're heads-down in our devices, we're missing out on the rich, face-to-face experiences that nourish our brains and souls. So, while we're all busy craning our necks to catch the latest cat video or tweet from a celebrity llama, let's not forget that the real world is out there, waiting for us to look up, laugh, and enjoy the show! Oh, wait… let's start another movement, #LookUpandsee.

Listen, I am not saying you need to always speak to everybody. I hope instead to encourage you to be open even to casual connectivity with others as you go about your day. It does not mean sitting down with every person you pass and interviewing them until you can write their biography.

It may be as quick or simple as a smile,[25] eye contact, or a gentle head nod to say "I see you" to the person you are passing in the mall. Your brain will embrace the safety and rewards associated with being in a community. This, in turn, activates neurotransmitters that enhance our cognitive well-being, resilience, learning, and high performance.[26]

Where do you see opportunities to connect better with others? Study after study found that relationships are the only common denominator in finding long-term happiness.[27] Quality relationships trigger those neurotransmitters that fire off good chemicals in our brains. They create natural opportunities for a consistent connection. Once we decide to deliberately build more connectivity,

---

[25] Guéguen, N., & Gail, M. (2003). The effect of smiling on helping behavior: Smiling and good Samaritan behavior. *Communication Reports*.
[26] Brooks, M., Lovett, J., & Creek, S. (2013). Case Study in Focus: CA Technologies.
[27] Brill, P. (2014). Triumphs of Experience: The Men of the Harvard Grant Study. *Activities, Adaptation & Aging*.

our brains will immediately cue us to do things like smile more often.

Smiling is a small but mighty act. A hospital implemented a policy for the staff to smile whenever they were within 10 feet of someone else in the hallways.[28] Imagine the scene of endless corridors transformed into runways of beaming faces! It's like a perpetual wave of joy, with each smile sparking another. Amidst the hustle and bustle, these smiles became little beacons of hope and warmth to the brain, turning a sterile hospital environment into a gallery of grins. It was a beautiful reminder that sometimes, the simplest gestures can make a world of difference to the human brain.

The hospital's culture improved dramatically with this policy, including increased patient satisfaction. Smiles create community, even if just for a moment because they connect us to another person. Oh sure, sometimes you might have to force a smile.

Even involuntarily smiling can lead to positive cognitive benefits, though. Both voluntary and involuntary smiling arouse the same patterns of regional brain activity.[29] So, yes, when we are smiling, we boost our brain's resiliency. You've heard the saying, "Fake it until you make it." Our brains feed off of every smile.

The B-Plan

Let's connect some of what we have covered and add a few items into the framework that make it easy for your brain to recall. This will be another way for you to plan out the practical and tactical things that you can immediately start applying. These are

---

[28] Amedee, R. (2017). From the Editor's Desk: Well-Being in the Workplace.
[29] Ekman, P., & Davidson, R. (1993). Voluntary Smiling Changes Regional Brain Activity. *Psychological Science*.

tactics that we can leverage to daily train our brains. I call it the B-Plan. By following this B-Plan, we can choose to be aligned, be generous, be curious, and be grateful. Let's dive deeper into each of these strategies to build our best brain.

1- Be Aligned

Our purpose must be aligned with our priorities. Articulating your personal why naturally allows for alignment. When you have defined what matters to you and ordered your priorities, you will develop some clarity around your purpose. Align your decisions, tasks, thoughts, and efforts with that personal mission statement. When the things that you think, say, and do align with your WHY, your brain will begin to undergo a radical transformation.

Just like how every meeting, task, and assignment within a large corporation ought to align with the organization's values, goals, and objectives, so should your personal choices. You can also choose to align with the people that you work with. Align with the relationships in your life. As you build community, seek ways to help others to align with their needs. As everything falls into alignment with your why, you will move not only toward success but also toward eudemonic joy.

You can only get to alignment by dedicating time to reflect quietly on the critical questions we ask in the book. That reflection should lead to expressing your thoughts on paper and moving to conclusions that are right for you based on where you are now and your current stage in life. This will become a "living document" that you can revisit, and revise based on things you accomplish along the way. You may also find that you need to adjust your goals as you navigate and mature through each stage of life.

2- Be Generous

The more you get, the more you should give. When we turn into modern-day dragons, hoarding our treasures and growling at anyone who comes near, our chances of success drop faster than a clumsy knight in an oversized suit of armor. It's like trying to win a marathon while carrying a sack of gold, which, it turns out, is not the best brain strategy.

So, we need to set up some generosity guidelines. Think of them like a 'Share Your Toys' policy from kindergarten but for grown-ups. This way, we're more about giving high-fives than keeping everything to ourselves. After all, the more you give, the more you... well, don't have to rent a storage unit for all that extra stuff!

We must commit to personal parameters that encourage generosity so that we are focused on giving to others. Developing a sense of generosity helps to improve our outlook, resiliency, and ability to recover from stressors.[30] Be deliberate about giving generously of your time, knowledge, and resources, as this will aid in training your brain toward success, especially when dealing with challenges.[31]

In one study, they used functional magnetic resonance imaging (fMRI) to investigate the link between generosity and happiness. Researchers saw remarkable results as early as when participants made a promise to be generous.[32] As soon as you decide and commit to generosity, a neural response occurs immediately, benefiting your brain, outlook, and a sense of happiness.

---

[30] Rutter, M. (2012). Resilience as a dynamic concept. *Development and Psychopathology*
[31] Rutten, B., Hammels, C., Geschwind, N., Menne-Lothmann, C., Pishva, E., Schruers, K., Hove, D., Kenis, G., os, J., & Wichers, M. (2013). Resilience in mental health: linking psychological and neurobiological perspectives.
[32] Park, S. Q., Kahnt, T., Dogan, A., Strang, S., Fehr, E., & Tobler, P. N. (2017). A neural link between generosity and happiness.

So, I wonder if now is a good time for you to pause and think about your current levels of generosity and where you might have other opportunities to share your time, talents, and resources for the benefit of others.

3- Be Curious

As we have previously explored, asking questions is a skill that can be practiced and refined. For some of us, being curious about those around us occurs more naturally than it might for others. Yet, all of us can learn to do it better. Often, it is helpful to start with everyday conversations. How many conversations can you start today by asking a question and listening carefully to the answer?

Your brain responds to your act of curiosity with a sense of competence that helps to bridge your everyday experiences into a more stable personality trait.[33] Ultimately, the research reveals that curiosity improves not only relationships but also physical and mental resilience. Asking curious questions is a skill that you can learn and practice, just like any other skill. It is also a habit that you can establish and build for the benefit of your brain and well-being, just like any other habit.

Of course, once you ask, you must listen respectfully and intently, like a detective at a mystery novel convention. You might even have follow-up questions. In Western-educated countries, we're kind of famous for asking questions like we're tossing confetti everywhere and without much follow-through.

Take the classic, "How are you?" It is almost like a drive-by greeting. We continued moving in the direction we were walking

---

[33] Silvia, P., & Kashdan, T. (2009). Interesting things and curious people: Exploration and engagement as transient states and enduring strengths.

and never really intended to listen to their answer. Imagine if we actually stopped and listened?

We might find out that Bob from accounting is a weekend skydiving instructor, or that Karol in HR breeds prize-winning chihuahuas. Typically, though, in as much time as it takes for them to take a breath to respond, we are already halfway down the corridor. Imagine how much fun you could have watching people's reactions when you actually paused after asking, "How you doin'?" and waited intently for an answer.

When we adopt an attitude of curiosity, we must also embrace the principle that the person we are currently talking to is the most important person in the world at that moment. If we can lock that principle into our brains, our non-conscious mind will align our nonverbal signals in a way that revolutionizes how we come across to others. Improving your listening capabilities is very powerful for your business success.[34]

There was a speaker at a conference who said, "The future of leadership does not belong to the person with the most answers, but the leader with the most questions." Asking questions is how we maintain and grow in our agility and our ability to respond to situations quickly and insightfully. When we ask a good question and listen thoughtfully to the answer, we gain a shift in perspective. It expands our brain power. The most successful leaders of tomorrow are the most curious leaders of today.

Additionally, by adopting this "most important person principle," you positively impact your own brain to see others as more valuable. Thus, when you focus solely on the human in front of you, you change how you behave with them.[35] This competency

---

[34] Gias, S. (2020). A Conceptual Model of Listening Effectiveness and Agile Selling Behavior: Moderating Effect of E-Communication and Consumption Pattern.
[35] Rogers, C., & Farson, R. (2015). Active Listening.

not only increases your positive impact on relationships, but it also helps to counter brain damage that can occur from stressors and a negative outlook if we fail to build an attitude of curiosity.[36]

4- Be Grateful

The positive impact of gratitude on the human brain is significant. What physically happens in the brain is that gratitude leads to the secretion of dopamine. It's like that feeling you get after exercising, even when you really didn't want to start at all.

You know, the whole "I'd rather be binge-watching a show with a bag of chips" mood. It's the cold, dark morning that you want to spend snuggled in bed instead of lacing up your sneakers. Yet, you exercise anyway. By the time you finish your workout, bam! You discover that your brain is already throwing a dopamine party, and you're suddenly feeling like a superhero.

Laughter works the same way in activating your dopaminergic system. Have you ever laughed so hard that you turned into a human fountain with a constant stream of tears running down your face? Maybe your sides ached like you did a thousand crunches, or you caught the giggles and just could not stop, no matter how hard you tried. Remember that time when you laughed for so long that you forgot why you were laughing?

Laughing is, in fact, great medicine. That old saying is still true today. Interestingly, the top ways to legally trigger substantial dopamine release include exercise, deep laughter, and another activity I couldn't print in the book without issuing a warning on the front cover. I think you know what I mean!

---

[36] Khalid, N. (2018). Most of us consider being a good listener crucial for the success of any relationship. It is a quality that denotes how patient we are as people and how much we are willing to give to others.

When we focus on gratitude, we not only reframe and refocus our brain, but we also encourage the release of dopamine. We get the feeling that we've had a good laugh. A focus on gratitude also triggers the release of serotonin. When dopamine and serotonin combine, we feel a sense of happiness and increased well-being. According to the Mayo Clinic, there are many other benefits, including better sleep and a boost to your immune system.[37]

Gratitude helps to refill your pitcher. Gratitude should be a daily focus for all of us. Whether you keep a gratitude journal or use it as a focal point for your meditation or quiet time, think about how you can deliberately build this into your daily routine.

---

[37] Mayo Clinic. Can expressing gratitude improve your mental, physical health? (2022)

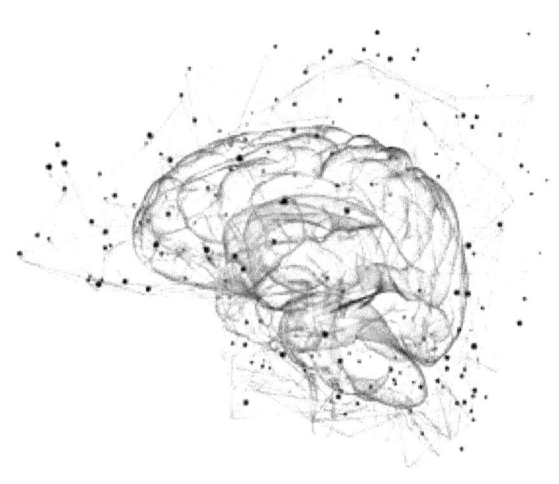

"One can choose to go back toward safety or forward toward growth. Growth must be chosen again and again; fear must be overcome again and again."

- Abraham Maslow

Chapter 4

Choose Your Program

Messaging

We are bombarded with daily messages that are deliberately designed to influence our brains. That is why choosing your personal purpose, which we explored in the previous chapter, is essential to cognitive focus and success. After choosing your purpose, the next step is to choose your program.

Think of your brain as if it were a computer. They both need programming software to operate, calculate, and produce results. Your brain is constantly being bombarded with sources of programming. If you are not deliberate about programming your own brain, you can be sure that other sources will provide programming code that may or may not align with who you really want to be and how you want to show up with others.

When you follow the B-Plan, you will experience an increase in dopamine. The scary thing is that platforms like social media are designed to do the exact same thing. Countless articles and documentaries reveal the deliberate attempt by social media platforms to influence your brain.

They want to manipulate you to stay longer on the platform, click where they want you to click, and think about what the algorithms want you to think about. That is why social media is so addictive; it trains your brain to yearn for more dopamine so that, over time, we need more than we did before. Unfortunately, the long-term impact of social media addiction on the brain is significant and can lead to depression, self-harm, and anxiety.[38]

Think of an optical illusion in which multiple pictures can be seen from the same image. Optical illusions leverage our brain's tendency to complete patterns and fill in the gaps. There is a classic one of an old woman and a young woman in the same image.

Since our brains love to jump to conclusions and fill in the blanks, you usually spot one of the ladies immediately. Then, someone comes along and points out the other lady in the picture. They might say, "Hey, see how the old lady's nose is actually the young lady's chin?" Suddenly, it's like a lightbulb moment… "Aha! There she is!"

The funny thing is that you can't unsee both ladies once you see them. It's like they're both photobombing each other forever in that picture. Every time you look, you'll see the old lady and the young lady hanging out together and wonder how you ever missed them in the first place! Once you see something, you can't unsee it.

While these popular optical illusions can often be fun, visual imagery can work against us when it adds stress to our cognitive processing. We view negative images in bulk through news, media, and various sources. We are constantly bombarded by images that elevate our stress to unhealthy levels. Researchers tell us that this makes us anti-social and less productive.

---

[38] Basha, K., & Chavan, V. (2022). Impact of Social Media Psychologically on high School Students. *International Journal of All Research Education & Scientific Methods.*

Social media is only one of many sources that try to influence your brain deliberately. Remember, your brain is constantly bombarded with messages and has to filter through what is important. At one point in my leadership journey, I worked as a program manager with a major cable company. It was exciting to be in this industry as we transitioned from analog capability to digital technology.

When we functioned on an analog system, I would have to take one channel off in order to put a new channel on. My role required that I research each cable channel, its popularity, and its relevance to the customers in our region of the country. It was through that experience that I learned how much money a popular, growing entertainment channel was spending on research about how to influence children. I was shocked!

Although their content was not created for children, or even appropriate for them, they spent excessive amounts of money on learning how to influence children's thinking. They knew that if they converted casual viewers into dedicated followers at a young age, they would secure long-term popularity.

I would later discover how frequently this practice was used across many other networks. Knowledge of the intentional targeting of children's brains was a paradigm shift for me, as I used to think that networks were solely about entertainment. Yet, the truth is that so many are actually focused on influencing our thinking and our choices.

We may think of these programmers as providing us solely with an entertainment outlet, but many of them think of their platform as a way to influence your beliefs, decisions, and outlook. Many, many, many studies have been done to better understand the effects of television programming, especially on our children.[39] [40] Some of the research has focused on the good that comes from specific educational programming. Others, like a study in Norway, reveal that television programming can actually contribute to a reduction in your overall intelligence.[41]

Our persistent journey into the online and broadcast world is contributing to our stress load and reduced cognitive capacity. There is a lot of research examining how the internet acutely impacts many of our cognitive processing systems, including attention, memory, and critical thinking.[42] We live in a rapidly evolving digital age, and avoiding the online and media world may not be a realistic expectation. What we want to do instead is to be deliberate about mitigating it and maintain an awareness of how we can be influenced.

We must deliberately choose when and how much media intake we may want to tolerate. For example, I only listen to the news at specific times of the day, and I only listen for short periods of time. I will access multiple sources to try and mitigate the bias associated with any one news outlet, and I desperately avoid the news early in the morning or late at night. I only watch on-demand or pre-recorded shows at night that make me feel good, such as a comedy or a well-produced drama that stays away from highly controversial topics and does not have foul language or graphic

---

[39] Singer, M., Miller, D., Guo, S., Flannery, D., Frierson, T., & Slovak, K. (1999). Contributors to Violent Behavior Among Elementary and Middle School Children.
[40] Hapkiewicz, W. (1979). Children's reactions to cartoon violence. *Journal of Clinical Child and Adolescent Psychology*.
[41] Hernæs, Ø., Markussen, S., & Røed, K. (2016). Television, cognitive ability, and high school completion (IZA DP No. 9645). *Bonn: Forschungsinstitut zur Zukunft der Arbeit Institute for the Study of Labor*.
[42] Firth, J., Torous, J., Stubbs, B., Firth, J. A., Steiner, G. Z., Smith, L., Alvarez-Jimenez, M., Gleeson, J., Vancampfort, D., Armitage, C. J., & Sarris, J. (2019). The "online brain": How the Internet may be changing our cognition. *World Psychiatry*.

scenes. I am intentional about what I allow to influence my brain, and when I allow it.

The "time of the day strategy" mentioned above also applies to social media access. I rarely engage with my phone or laptop late at night or within the first 30-60 minutes of my morning. The only exception is if it is part of my morning meditative and reflective process. Then I have other boundaries in place to help facilitate using it only for that purpose. When I finally give in and hop onto social media later in the day, I hit myself with the big question: "Am I here to give or to get?"

If the answer is "to get," I know I'm just there for a quick dopamine fix. Then, since I know I'm on a dopamine treasure hunt, I can act sort of like a kid looking for hidden candy. It is all about seeing if my latest post hit the jackpot with likes or if it took a nosedive into the land of digital obscurity. I am deliberate about my decision to engage.

I'll admit that, like so many others, sometimes I want a sweet hit of that brain candy. Doing this every now and then is okay. It does not make us bad humans. It only makes us human.

What we must remember is that too much of something can quickly become bad. Thinking about how often I allow myself to indulge in the dopamine release helps to regulate addictive patterns that would otherwise emerge. Leveraging the question about giving or getting is a great guide to evaluating my decisions to access a social media platform. Eventually, I find myself going days without accessing social media sites, mainly because it does not often cross my mind anymore. I find that my brain remains focused on things that are much more important to me.

Alternatively, if the answer is, "to give" when I do jump online, then that means I am going onto social media to post something that will help or support others. I might be posting a short article to help folks solve a challenge, or maybe I recently discovered stress-reducing research that I want to share.

I find that a ratio of 3-1 seems to work well. I need to log in "to give" at least three times as much as I log in "to get." That ratio, coupled with the ability to go days without a need to access social media at all, are the guardrails I use in my personal life to manage the negative influential effects of social media.

Let's be Deliberate About Being Deliberate

When we understand the influence that the world around us seeks in our lives, we have to make deliberate choices. We must decide what we want to influence us and build our brain so that it does not give in to the pressure of marketing and media. If we are not deliberate about choosing our program, then our program will be chosen for us by others.

We often do not realize it, and that is precisely what advertisers and influencers desire for us. They have a different definition of success than we do, and they want to implement their products, services, and worldviews in our lives. In the same way that large organizations can suffer from mission drift, or the idea that they get caught up in everyday processes and drift away from their original mission, we can drift away from our personal purpose.

We have to choose to think through things that we often accept as commonplace. I am originally from the Caribbean, so there are some things about the United States and our neighbors that were quite confusing to me and forced me to think. For instance, in America, we've collectively agreed that Mondays are about as enjoyable as a root canal. Seriously, it is practically a national pastime to gripe about them. How did we end up in this

Monday misery club? It is a well-known moniker. Why is that? How did that become a social construct?

It has gotten to the point where people start feeling the Sunday blues because they know Monday is lurking around the corner. Before you know it, Sunday itself gets caught in the crossfire, and both days turn into a double feature of "suckiness." We don't only do this with Monday; we do this all throughout the week. We've all had *that* coworker that comes into the office with a loud, low voice on Wednesday, yelling, "hump day!"

Let's not forget about poor Tuesday, stuck between Monday and "hump day." It's like the forgotten middle child who's developing a severe case of day-of-the-week psychosis! It's feeling left out, unloved, and questioning its existence. "Am I not special enough for a catchy nickname?"

Friday has become its own beast with mottos like T.G.I.F. and Fri-yay. Yet, do you ever notice how Fridays at work can sometimes be less productive than a sloth on a hammock? We are all just mentally speed-dialing the weekend, thinking about those beachside margaritas while the poor tasks on our desks languish in neglect. We assign social value to days of the week for virtually no reason. Imagine what it does for your brain to constantly dread Mondays.

In the universe I created in my own head, every day is Thursday! There is no social construct around the days, so you can enjoy every day. It eliminates the dread of particular days of the week. It is good for your brain to not automatically throw away every Monday.

Friends, I ask you to join my revolution. Imagine the audacity to start a social rebellion where every day of the week sparkles brighter than a disco ball at a dance party! I am not the first person to proclaim the absurdity of tossing every Monday into the bad day-of-the-week pile, so let's all band together. Let's put an end to this blatant weekday discrimination.

Can you visualize it? We're armed with coffee cups, matching t-shirts, and quirky motivational posters declaring war on the Monday blues. We'll storm into the office on Monday, high-fiving coworkers and shouting, "Happy Thursday, everybody." Folks, it's time to make Mondays so awesome that even Fridays will be jealous!

Grab your "Let's save Mondays" battle gear, a smile, and a positive attitude, and let's embark on a revolution of epic proportions. Together, we shall conquer the Monday mayhem and turn it into a day of pure awesomeness! Who is with me?!?

The teams that work for me and with me already know that I have personally adopted this philosophy. Someone might ask, "Hey, how is your Tuesday going?" And I typically reply, "I don't know because, in my mind, today is Thursday." This strategy is known as reframing.

Cognitive reframing is the process in which we choose to change how we think about an event, situation, emotion, or idea. Reframing allows the brain to interpret an experience more positively. This practice allows your brain to focus on how your thinking is arousing certain feelings and behaviors, thus more easily determining which thoughts are not helpful. This is powerful for turning some of our self-talk from negative to positive.[43]

We are surrounded by so many false constructs that we have simply accepted as truth and reality. In addition to buying into the universal law that Mondays are the root of all evil, we have come to believe in a host of other fallacies. How about the ever-popular '3-

---

[43] Marasigan, Portia. (2019). USING BRIEF COGNITIVE RESTRUCTURING AND COGNITIVE DEFUSION TECHNIQUES TO COPE WITH NEGATIVE THOUGHTS. Social Values and Society.

Second Rule,' the widely accepted theory that if you drop your food and scoop it up within three seconds, it's still fit for royalty. Spoiler alert: Your floor isn't a magic germ-free zone, no matter how fast your reflexes are.

Then there's the old saying, "Lightning never strikes the same place twice." Tell that to the poor Empire State Building, which might roll its eyes (if it had any), considering how often it gets zapped. On a few rare occasions, One World Trade Center and the Empire State Building were struck at the same time. Yipes!

So, as we wade through these amusing misconceptions, let's remember to take them with a grain of salt, or maybe a whole shaker, depending on your taste preference. Sometimes, our belief in a false construct can be something widely and socially perpetuated. In other situations, it can emerge from our personal journeys, learnings, and experiences.

What we believe is reality impacts our brains and can often cause unnecessary stress. Every now and then, we may need to pause and think about what we are thinking about and occasionally ask ourselves if we really know this to be true. Pay specific attention to the potentially false constructs that impact not only our behaviors but also the way we feel about ourselves and others.

Cognitive reframing, sometimes referred to as cognitive restructuring, stimulates the brain to secrete different neurotransmitters that lead to more pleasant and hopeful feelings, thus improving brain capability. Our thinking patterns create biochemical reactions that influence how we feel physically.

That is why Mondays "feel" stressful while turning every day into Thursday "feels" optimistic, hopeful, fun, and more enjoyable. If Tuesdays are your favorite day of the week, then personalize the mantra to say: "Every day is a Tuesday." Think of it as pouring a little more into your pitcher versus pouring more out.

That is what it means to be deliberate. Let's choose to be intentional about reframing the negative influences that we can, eliminating them when possible, and mitigating those we cannot get rid of. Retraining your brain to deliberately filter out negative social messaging extends to every arena of our lives.

The other deliberate step we need to take is to revise our daily schedule. Where are you creating daily opportunities to relax and rejuvenate? The research clearly shows that we need to spend time deliberately focusing on maintaining a sense of optimism and spending time in environments of social support. Whether it is a community group, meditation, or another activity, we all need to have a daily process that allows us to celebrate and acknowledge the good things in our lives and about our lives.

The final component of being deliberate is to apply the principles discussed in this book. Reading it is not going to be enough. You will need to be intentional about writing out specific actions you plan to take. Then, hold yourself accountable to do what you promised yourself you would do. By writing out your goals and sharing them with someone else, you also activate additional components of the brain, allowing them to contribute to your success. Capturing your goals in writing is associated with a significant increase in your well-being and reduced stress.[44] [45]

---

[44] King, L. (2001). The Health Benefits of Writing about Life Goals. *Personality and Social Psychology Bulletin*.
[45] Dietrich, J., Jokisaari, M., & Nurmi, J. (2012). Work-related goal appraisals and stress during the transition from education to work ☆. *Journal of Vocational Behavior*.

Reset

The human brain needs to have time to reset. There are a number of strategies to help our brains take a break to reset. When we use rest to reset, we can build a brain that aligns and realigns with our personal purpose. With rest, we remind ourselves of what is important and how to filter out what is not important. Rest can occur in a couple of different ways. We all have a rest network in the brain. The rest network is active whether we are asleep or awake.

One form of rest is sleep. Everything about building your better brain starts and stops with sleep! Sleep is a natural way to reset the brain. Sleep is also vital for effective cognitive functioning while you are awake, including the process of allostasis discussed earlier. Right now, I'm probably reminding you of Nana as we uncover her hidden genius as a neuroscientist. As she tucked you into bed, she always uttered her timeless mantra, "Make sure you get enough sleep; it's good for you."

Maybe she would add, "Early to bed, early to rise, makes you healthy, wealthy, and alert enough to find matching socks!" Little did you know, Grandma was championing the wonders of circadian rhythms and the cognitive benefits of a well-structured sleep schedule. Nothing else really matters if we are not giving the brain sufficient sleep.

During sleep cycles, the hippocampus becomes a hard-working part of the brain. It filters through the information from that day to decide what is essential. The hippocampus asks questions like, what needs to move to long-term memory? It is how we determine what is truly important and what gets categorized as a short-term thought or experience. The hippocampus activity while we rest is also contributing to our capacity for decision-making when awake.[46]

Since sleep is so critical to brain function, it makes sense that the stages directly before and after it are also crucial. So, what are you typically doing 20-30 minutes before bed? Unfortunately, for many of us, it is like inviting a gang of negative messages to a late-night party in our brains without a guard at the door.

Think about what you do before bed and upon waking. If you are like so many other people in North America, it probably involves a screen. We tend to sit in bed and scroll or let the television drone on. However, with phones and TVs come bad news, targeting marketing, and promotional pressure. You may be thinking, "Hey, who can resist the siren song of cat videos and social media drama, right?"

So, here's the deal: it is time to reclaim those precious bedtime moments. When you first wake up in the morning and right before you go to bed at night are optimal learning time frames. Since your brain is processing that information while you sleep, you can prime your brain before you go to bed. Let's kick those negative messages out of the sleepover and make way for dreams that don't involve media manipulation and social drama.

As you prepare to sleep, recognize this as a very vulnerable time of the day for your brain and be deliberate about what you will let enter. During this time of the evening, your brain is transitioning into Alpha waves, which is a relaxed and restful state. You are still awake and conscious, yet slowing down from the faster brain waves of a busy day. If we do this right, your Alpha brain wave state

---

[46] Schuck, N., & Niv, Y. (2019). Sequential replay of nonspatial task states in the human hippocampus.

should create a sense of calmness similar to what you might experience during meditation.

We naturally experience Alpha waves again when we first wake up. What does that look like for you? What is the first thing you do in the morning? Once again, if you reach for a phone, tablet, laptop, or remote control, you are already creating stress for your brain. You are actually forcing the brain out of the Alpha stage earlier than it would have if allowed to progress naturally.

Our brains transition through a series of waves as part of our waking cycle. When we are in a deep sleep state, we are experiencing beta waves. We then enter into a daydreaming state associated with theta waves.

After theta comes Alpha. Of the five types of brain waves, Alpha is right in the middle of them all. In this state, the flow between the conscious brain and the non-conscious brain is wide open. In the alpha stage, the brain is better able to regulate our sleep-wake cycles.[47] We want brain wave transitions to occur naturally, but when we reach for a device and access a screen, we force our brains to exit the important Alpha stage prematurely.

In the same way that we are deliberate about what we will do right before bed, we need to be intentional about what we will do when we first wake up. We want to allow our brains to fully benefit from this natural sense of calmness and relaxation. In doing so, we add a little more into our pitcher instead of starting our day by pouring some out.

Now, as a parent myself, I understand that some people don't always have complete control of their time when they first wake up. You can be peacefully dreaming of a world where alarm clocks

---

[47] Davis, H., Davis, P., Loomis, A., Harvey, E., & Hobart, G. (1937). CHANGES IN HUMAN BRAIN POTENTIALS DURING THE ONSET OF SLEEP.

don't exist when suddenly, your adorable little munchkins are yanking the blankets off you, the dogs are in full-on bark symphony mode, and there is a mysterious Lego blockade at the foot of your bed. However, to the extent that we can, we need to be deliberate about establishing a routine about how we start our days so that it leads to a better brain.

Maybe that means instituting family routines that give the children time in their rooms with designated activities in the mornings. Maybe that means developing a habit of waking up earlier so that you can carve out 20 minutes of "me-time." What changes would you need to make to manage your "Alpha-time" at the start of each day?

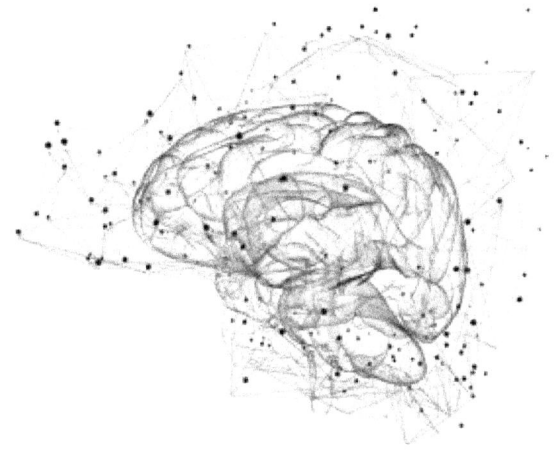

"As human beings, our greatness lies not so much in being able to remake the world – that is the myth of the atomic age – as in being able to remake ourselves."

– Mahatma Gandhi

Chapter 5

Choose Your Place

Environment

Your environment has a significant impact on brain function. Although it is essential that you choose your purpose and choose your program, it is also necessary to carefully choose your place. We are defining "place" as the physical environment that you choose to be in, as well as those whom you choose to be around. Let's start by focusing on going outside to let your brain play.

Not everyone can choose the parameters for the environment that they work in. We can, however, choose to introduce brain-friendly elements into parts of our day. For example, cognitive research reveals that a walk in nature boosts activity in the region of the brain that helps us to process stress and decreases activity in the amygdala.[48]

In fact, just simply inserting a walk, even if it is around the block and not necessarily on a nature trail, will also yield positive

---

[48] Sudimac, S., Sale, V., & Kühn, S. (2022).
How nature nurtures: Amygdala activity decreases as the result of a one-hour walk in nature. *Molecular Psychiatry*.

cognitive benefits.[49] It does not have to be strenuous. I sometimes will take a slow walk outside while conducting a coaching session with a leader over the phone. It improves my thinking, creativity, and mood.

So many well-known people reportedly incorporated walking into their work-day routines. Henry David Thoreau, Ernest Hemingway, and JK Rowling have attributed some of their creative success to talking walks. Steve Jobs and Nikola Tesla were famous for using walks to increase their creativity and problem-solving skills. Beethoven would often meet Goethe to go for a walk. Now, that is a combination that fascinates me!

Imagine a brilliant composer taking a walk with a remarkable poet! Oh, how I would have loved to hear just one of those conversations as one idea emerged after another. Beethoven would be like, "Hey, Goethe, what if we compose a sonata about the beauty of sunsets?" And Goethe would reply, "Ah, Ludwig, I've got just the lines to capture the colors of the evening sky!" If only we could've eavesdropped on one of those epic chats, right? It would be like witnessing a cosmic collision of creativity and culture with a side of picturesque park scenery near the German border! I digress...

---

[49] Zhou, Y., Zhang, Y., Hommel, B., & Zhang, H. (2017). The Impact of Bodily States on Divergent Thinking: Evidence for a Control-Depletion Account. *Frontiers in Psychology*.

Physical Space

Many factors contribute to your physical space: temperature, lighting, sounds, textures, aromas, etc. I feel like practically every residential college student has had that passive-aggressive college roommate who was your nemesis during the unpleasant game of thermostat wars. I know I had a few.

You set it to your desired temperature, only to return an hour later and see it's been adjusted. Some folks want to turn the room into a polar ice cave, while others envision a tropical paradise. Count me in on Team Tropical. After all, I was born in the Caribbean.

The point is that we all have preferences about what makes us most comfortable. My daughter likes her device screens set to the dimest possible setting. If she shows me her phone, she has to turn the brightness up before I can read anything. If I hand her my phone, she complains of it hurting her eyes. My brain would not function optimally if I worked under her ideal conditions, and vice versa. We all need to deliberately control our workspace as much as we can.

Maybe you feel the most productive when you're diffusing peppermint essential oils rumored to promote happiness. You become so productive that you feel like you could organize a herd of cats in a fish market! Maybe, for you, it is about having the right chair that does not make your back ache. Perhaps that small, portable heater for under your desk is now sounding like a really good idea.

You may need to invest in a soft sweater, different indoor shoes, or the right coffee mug to warm your hands. By the way, warm hands have a distinct effect on brain function and decision-making. Research studies have shown that when our hands are warmed by a gentle source such as a cup of hot beverage or a warming pad, it impacts our perceptions of others, improves decision-making, and positively influences our emotional state.[50] The researchers discovered that if you are holding something warm, you are most likely to perceive someone else as warm and thus behave in a more friendly and generous manner.

Whether it is the heat from a warm beverage or the temperature in the room, your brain will function much better under some conditions versus others. The ideal room temperature will vary by person, so I can't give you a thermostat setting that will be best for your brain. We all have to experiment to discover what is ideal (but please don't tell your roommate or significant other that the experiment was my idea).

Some research studies have shown that a room can become so warm that it will slow down your executive functioning skills. Other research reveals that a comfortably cool room improves cognitive performance. That being said, the research is clear that above 90 degrees or below 50 degrees will negatively affect your cognitive performance.[51] As long as you keep your thermostat within that range, you should be able to find the temperature that is ideal for you.

I was surprised to learn that there was research on how the ceiling height in our rooms impacts our creativity. The term "cathedral effect" emerged in a 2007 published study. The study revealed that rooms with higher ceilings promoted increased creative and abstract thinking compared to rooms with lower

---

[50] Lawrence E. Williams, John A. Bargh, Experiencing Physical Warmth Promotes Interpersonal Warmth.Science. (2008)
[51] Varjo, J., Hongisto, V., Haapakangas, A., Maula, H., Koskela, H., & Hyönä, J. (2015). Simultaneous effects of irrelevant speech, temperature and ventilation rate on performance and satisfaction in open-plan offices. *Journal of Environmental Psychology*.

ceilings. The space created by a higher ceiling gives the brain a sense of freedom to explore a broader thinking canvas.

Additionally, we tend to experience more positive emotions in spacious environments than we do in tighter spaces.[52] The more creative you want to be, the higher your ceiling ought to be. If you have to do detailed analytical work, a 10x10 office will do the job, that is, assuming that you are not claustrophobic.

You will want to find another space if you have to do creative work. Try the cafeteria, where the ceilings tend to be higher and the room bigger. If you work from home, try moving to the living room area if that ceiling is higher than your home office.

I'm not suggesting that you knock out your home office ceiling and replace it with a two-story A-frame structure. While that would be nice, it may not be financially responsible. How about we explore opportunities to take your laptop to the back patio when working on specific tasks that could benefit from a creativity boost?

Plants have a powerful impact on all of us. Bringing the outdoors into our workspace can help immensely. We ask our brains to spend approximately 85% of our time indoors. This is one of the reasons why I choose to focus on cognitive functionality and its relationship to our physical working environment. Research tells us that indoor plants help to reduce our stress.[53] Plants can also improve your sense of well-being and better recovery from things that drain your pitcher.[54]

---

[52] Stamps A. E. (2010). Effects of permeability on perceived enclosure and spaciousness. *Environ. Behav.*
[53] Lee, M. S., Lee, J., Park, B. J., & Miyazaki, Y. (2015). Interaction with indoor plants may reduce psychological and physiological stress by suppressing autonomic nervous system activity in young adults: a randomized crossover study. *Journal of physiological anthropology*
[54] Shibata, S., & Suzuki, N. (2001). Effects of indoor foliage plants on subjects' recovery from mental fatigue. *North American Journal of Psychology.*

Some of the benefits of indoor plants come from the relationship we develop in taking care of them, as well as the aesthetic pleasure. Just visually seeing them yields immediate brain benefits.[55] Even fake plants can bring some benefits to the brain.

Maybe reading this reminds you of how you failed at keeping plants alive in the past. Or perhaps there are other reasons why real plants will not work for you at this time. The good news is that you can still enjoy brain benefits from artificial plants in your environment. What adjustments can you implement in your physical space to help your brain do its best work?

When

Beyond making simple changes to our physical environment, we can also adjust when we do our best work. Although some people consider themselves night owls, we are at our best decision-making capacity in the morning. The period of time after you wake up is your most productive. One study of chess players found that we make slower and more accurate decisions in the morning, and we make faster but less accurate decisions later in the day.[56]

Since our cognitive capacity has not yet been drained, we are able to make some of our best choices within hours of being awake. If you are like me, you might like to postpone some of your more demanding tasks, but that is not the best thing for our brains. I confess, though, that we are painting with a pretty wide brush by applying this principle to everyone.

---

[55] Jeong, J., & Park, S. (2021). Physiological and Psychological Effects of Visual Stimulation with Green Plant Types. *International Journal of Environmental Research and Public Health*.
[56] Leone, M. J., Fernandez Slezak, D., Golombek, D., & Sigman, M. (2017). Time to decide: Diurnal variations on the speed and quality of human decisions. *Cognition*.

Now, you might be wondering, as I did, "Wait, what about night owls like me?" I may feel a little slump in the late afternoon, but then I get going again after dinner. Does this principle apply to us night owls? Before I answer that, let's rethink our narrative about morning versus evening people types. Traditionally, we have categorized people into the popular chronotype categories of night owls or early birds. Yet, the research insists that we expand that thinking.

Research shows us that there may be as many as four chronotypes, and most people can instinctively identify which one they are.[57] One expert refers to these as bears, wolves, lions, and dolphins.[58] Lions are up early and full of energy. According to the author, they account for about 15-20 percent of us.

About 50 percent of us are bears whose sleep and wake cycle aligns with the solar cycle, so they get 7-8 hours of sleep each night. Wolfs are closely aligned with our traditional definition of "night owls." 10-15 percent of us land in this category, where we get a higher energy level in the early evening. If you struggle with insomnia and consider yourself a light sleeper, then you would be a dolphin. Only 10 percent of people land here.

There are a host of assessments already in use to help people identify their chronotype if they don't already know it. It is important to note that chronotypes are not about your personality but more about your biology. Our daily biological patterns are tied to our internal clock. That clock is mastered by a part of the

---

[57] Putilov, Arcady & Marcoen, Nele & Neu, Daniel & Pattyn, Nathalie & Mairesse, Olivier. (2019). There is more to chronotypes than evening and morning types: Results of a large-scale community survey provide evidence for high prevalence of two further types. Personality and Individual Differences.

[58] The Power of When: Discover Your Chronotype--and the Best Time to Eat Lunch, Ask for a Raise, Have Sex, Write a Novel, Take Your Meds, and More. (2016) by Michael Breus PhD.

hypothalamus called the suprachiasmatic nucleus (SCN). Since we are all so very biologically different, the best times for our brains can vary.

So, the idea that we make our best decisions in the morning will still be valid for most of us, though it can change from one person to the other. Looking across the landscape of research, I believe that the vast majority of you reading this book will find the morning to be your best time for cognitive decision-making processing, with later in the day yielding some of your best creativity time.

The key here is to identify and understand what part of the day allows for your peak cognitive performance. While I am a traditional night owl, my best professional performance time has always been before noon. As I get older, I notice that this peak performance window has become even more distinct.

Glorification of busyness, no matter what time of day, is another false construct that I have seen poison the thinking of many leaders that I have coached. There is a sense that busyness is the equivalent of earning a medal of valor. Then, I remembered that at one point in my own career, I lived by that motto as well.

Companies used to hand out medals for busyness like it was an Olympic sport. "Look at me; I'm juggling fourteen tasks while hopping on one leg!" became the unofficial motto in office corridors. Executives prided themselves on a calendar so packed that it made Tetris look like child's play. We all got so caught up in this whirlwind of constant activity, tying our self-worth and value to how busy people thought we were. It was like being in a bizarre reality show where the prize was a pat on the back and an extra-large slice of stress.

We think we are being super productive, but in reality, our cognitive capacity is doing the limbo and wondering how low it can go. Meanwhile, science is over there, waving its hands, telling us that a few brain breaks a day can make us healthier, happier, and actually more productive. They are not just nice-to-haves; they're must-haves.

Imagine that! It's like finding out that eating chocolate could help you lose weight. Okay, so that last sentence may not be true. What is truthful, though, is discovering that sitting quietly for ten minutes could be way more valuable than an hour of frantic email typing. It is a bit like finding out that taking a pit stop in a NASCAR race can actually help you win it.

A daily schedule filled with endless meetings stresses the brain. To allow your brain time and space to reset, recharge, and excel, we must get our brains out of this continuous beta wave cycle. The lesson that I had to learn so many years ago was that when our brains get a chance to breathe, we're not just better leaders; we're like superheroes with enhanced brainpower. Who doesn't want to be a superhero without the spandex, right? We all must find daily strategies to cycle out of constant beta waves.

Think about 10-15 minutes of listening to your favorite feel-good music or taking a brief stroll. What else could you do? These daily integrations are some of the most effective ways to reintegrate and rejuvenate your brain. What brain break habits can you incorporate into your regular daily rhythm? It is all about deliberately refilling our pitchers throughout the day instead of pouring out until we have nothing left to give.

Additionally, early morning sunlight powers the brain[59]. That is yet another reason why the morning is the best time for most of us to make crucial decisions. What opportunities do you have to get outside early in the morning, even for a few minutes?

Personal Board of Trustees

Warning: Another Itchy Moment is approaching.

It has been said that we are simply a culmination of the five people that we spend the most time with. In the research world, there exists quite a debate about that principle. Some question the principle because they claim that we are influenced by way more than just five people. Other social influence scientists simply don't like to assign a hard number to the principle.

We all pretty much agree, though, that you and I are deeply influenced by the people in our social circles. Maybe it is four, or perhaps it is seven people. One Harvard social psychologist states that those we habitually hang out with will determine as much as 95 percent of our success… or failure.

In the same way that corporations form a board of directors to help guide them to success, think about our need for a Personal Board of Trustees to support our personal mission statement. Others refer to them as a personal board of directors. I prefer the term Board of Trustees because whether we like it or not, we are trusting these people to shape our thinking, values, goals, and behaviors.

One dictionary defines the Board of Trustees as "an appointed or elective board that supervises the affairs of a public or private

---

[59] Blume, C., Garbazza, C., & Spitschan, M. (2019). Effects of light on human circadian rhythms, sleep and mood. *Somnologie : Schlafforschung und Schlafmedizin = Somnology : sleep research and sleep medicine.*

organization." I like this definition because it is a choice, not necessarily conscious, we make to give this group of people private influence that will impact how we show up publicly. These people impact your cognitive capacity and your ability to be a high performer. They are shaping you. The people you surround yourself with matter greatly.

We tend to be socially attracted to people who are very similar to us. No matter what age we are, all of us, to some extent, care about what other people think of us. Consequently, those we spend the most time with will alter our habits, perspectives, and behaviors.[60] Before reading the next paragraph, please take a moment to write down the three to five people with whom you voluntarily spend the most time.

As you reflect on the list you just created, put a checkmark next to each name representing someone who is usually positive and uplifting.

Put an X next to the names of those who are generally bitter, angry, and negative. Maybe they are constantly talking about a group of other people in an angry way. Maybe every other day is filled with bitter political monologues. Maybe their sarcasm always places you or someone you care about at the center of their humor.

Place another checkmark next to the names that support your personal mission.

Place another check mark next to the names of those who typically leave you feeling good after interacting with them.

This evaluative process is the start of understanding what changes you may need to make to your board of trustees. The X

---

[60] Social networks and neural receptivity to persuasive health messages. Pandey P, Kang Y, Cooper N, O'Donnell MB, Falk EB. Health Psychol. 2021

marks the spot for the Grinches and the Negativity Ninjas, who seem to have made bitterness their side hustle. They're the ones whose conversations are like a rollercoaster of sour emotions. It's okay for our friends to have a bad day. They do not get an X next to their name just for having one bad day. We need to worry about the ones who have bad days like it is a way of life. Week after week.

We have all come across "those people." The "Eternal Grumbler" who could turn winning the lottery into a lamentation! You half-expect them to complain about finding a hundred-dollar bill on the sidewalk. I can hear them now, "Oh great, now I have to carry all this cash!" Come on y'all, life is too short to be surrounded by X's.

This translates into our work relationships as well. While we may not be able to choose our teammates or our bosses, we can choose to develop other positive relationships with colleagues in the workplace. Our brains crave positive relationships at work like we crave the last donut in the break room. In fact, research tells us that if we have a healthy positive relationship in the workplace, it is equivalent to about a $150,000 raise.[61]

Now, hold your horses, my financially ambitious friend! If your knee-jerk reaction is to say, "Forget the friends, just hand me that cold hard cash," well, you might be missing the memo here. It is not the Benjamins that your brain needs; it is the sense of camaraderie and moral support when the coffee in the office tastes like dishwater. It is about someone standing by your side when you are trying to convince your boss that casual Fridays should include pajamas. Seriously though, when it comes to brain health, people with close, positive, and trusted confidants are more resilient,

---

[61] Powdthavee, N. (2008). Putting a price tag on friends, relatives, and neighbours: Using surveys of life satisfaction to value social relationships. *The Journal of Socio-Economics*

satisfied, and less likely to suffer from depression, according to the research.[62]

Whether in the office or in our social life, we must become intentional with whom we choose to spend our time. There is significant and powerful research to compel us to make this a priority. Surrounding ourselves with positive, encouraging people of good moral and ethical character helps to counteract the increasingly hostile and combative environment around us. These relationships change how your brain reacts to stress and are often a source for refilling your pitcher instead of draining it. Spending time with such a friend arouses regions of the brain associated with a positive self-view, motivation, and reward.[63]

Unfortunately, the opposite is true when we have negative and draining friendships. Poor-quality friendships have a more significant negative impact on our health than smoking does. We become twice as likely to die prematurely.[64] If you have someone on your Personal Board of Trustees who is constantly negative or does not support your core values, you need to fire them immediately.

---

[62] Choi, K. W., et al., *The American Journal of Psychiatry*. (2020)
[63] Güroğlu, B., *Child Development Perspectives*. (2022)
[64] *PLOS Medicine*. (2010)

"Twenty years from now, you will be more disappointed by the things that you didn't do than by the ones you did do. So, throw off the bowlines. Sail away from the safe harbor. Catch the trade winds in your sails. Explore. Dream. Discover."

- Mark Twain

Conclusion

Our brains are under constant pitcher-draining bombardments. This unpredictable, volatile world makes our brains extremely uncomfortable and stressed. So, we must take specific steps today to build our best brain in order to combat whatever will hit the fan tomorrow.

Equipping ourselves with the tools of this book will allow us to be deliberate and purposeful. Deliberate decisions can defend against Brain Drain so that we can lean into accelerating our success. Remember, if YOU don't program your brain, someone else will.

Your physical environment, the people you surround yourself with, and the constant input into your brain can be filtered through your personal purpose, subsequently helping to center your choices and catapult you into your success. You can develop habits that rejuvenate your brain.

It all starts with your decision to do some things differently. The habits you create today will equip your brain to handle the surprises of tomorrow.

Now that you're armed with a neuroscience-based model of Purpose, Program, and Place, let's get started in building your best brain!

About The Edwards Groups, LLC

The Edwards Group, began as a vibrant corporation in New York, housing an innovative trio: an advertising agency, a video production company, and a consulting firm, all in one corporate building. This powerhouse quickly garnered a prestigious client list, boasting major corporations like Smith Corona, Rubbermaid, and Cellular One.

With a slight name adjustment, now known as The Edwards Groups, LLC, (TEG) stands out for its exceptional presentations, captivating audiences so effectively that they're often left wanting more. With a commitment to delivering value beyond expectations, it's no surprise that over 80% of their clients are repeat collaborators.

TEG is also home to Leadershipopedia. An online resource of continuous positive reminders and reinforcement information for leaders. Whether it is your official title or not, we believe that leadership is action and not necessarily a title.

So, in a world that bombards us with negativity, we want to push back on that and provide you with a continuous source of positive energy, reinforcement, teaching and reminding.

TEG's expertise extends to training speakers, blending neuroscience with effective communication techniques. This unique approach empowers other speakers to create a lasting positive impact. The group's success in this domain is further highlighted by their publishing division, which has already released a book on the subject, with another insightful publication specifically for speakers, is on the way.

Visit **www.edwardsgroup.org** to discover the essence of The Edwards Group – a beacon of innovation and excellence in the corporate communication world, dedicated to accelerating your success!

More about John

John speaks weekly to audiences from around the globe. He was the top-ranked facilitator at the Center for Leadership Excellence for an unprecedented five years in a row! His insights aren't just heard; they're sought after, earning him the honor of Chairmanship for a U.S. Department of Justice initiative and leadership advisory roles requested by not one, not two, but three New York State Governors.

But wait, there's more! John is not just a speaker; he's a Master Trainer tasked with the noble duty of training other professional presenters. Imagine that—a trainer of trainers!

Ready for a dose of John's infectious energy and wisdom? Book him for your next conference, workshop, or seminar.

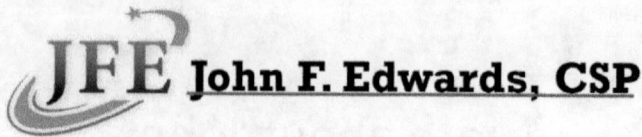
John F. Edwards, CSP

Dive deeper into his world and discover free resources at **www.getmotivationalspeaker.com**

and connect with him on LinkedIn at **www.linkedin.com/in/john-f-edwards/**

Use special code: **BYBB** *for our website promotions and free resources.*

NOTES

NOTES

NOTES

NOTES

NOTES

NOTES

NOTES

NOTES

NOTES

NOTES

NOTES

NOTES

www.ingramcontent.com/pod-product-compliance
Lightning Source LLC
Chambersburg PA
CBHW060045230426
43661CB00004B/663